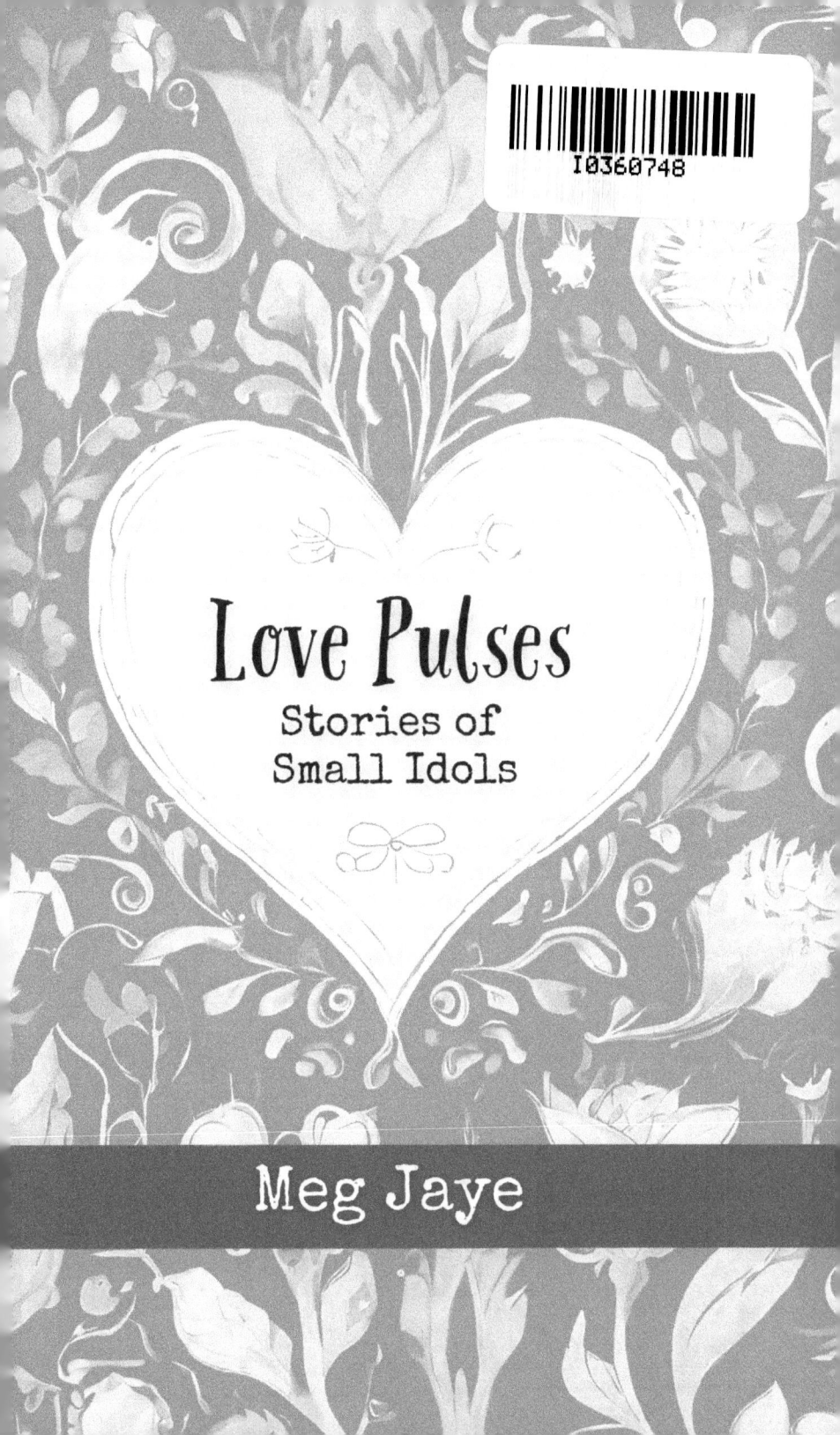

All rights reserved. No part of this book may be reproduced in any form on or by an electronic or mechanical means, including information storage and retrieval systems, without permission in writing from the publisher, except by a reviewer who may quote brief passages in a review.

© 2024 by Megan J. Padden

ISBN 978-1-7379849-5-5 (e-book)
ISBN 978-1-7379849-4-8 (paperback)

Published by Our Wisdom Leads Press
www.OurWisdomLeads.com

OUR WISDOM LEADS PRESS

TABLE OF CONTENTS

Author's Note 1

Innocence
Nostalgia 5
Evolution of an Artist 6
Unnamed 9

Crusades
The Sunflower 13
The Queen's Battle Cry 14
State of the Nation 18
Gentlemen on the Hill 20
Give Them Their Flowers 22

Spice
Cacophony's Clutch 25
Ascended 26
Expiration Date 27
Southbound Train 28
The Ego's Silent Departure 30
Amidst the Pieces of the Cerebral Realm 32

Healing
Resentment's Reprieve 37
Prescription for Healing 38
Wishes for Redemption 39

Anticipation
Searching for Home 43
Shallow Waters 45

The Odyssey -- 47
Harvesting Quandaries ------------------------------- 49

Desire

Love's Reverie --- 53
Burning Desire -- 55
The Rapture of Venus --------------------------------- 57
Trepidation --- 58
Love Pulses --- 59
Fireflies --- 60
Aphrodite's Inferno ------------------------------------ 61
Cryospheric Atrium ------------------------------------ 62

Sweet

Breath of Life: Love's Regeneration ---------------- 65
Inked in Sight --- 67
Persephone's Dream ----------------------------------- 69
Wanted -- 71
Morning Jazz -- 72
Autumn Esperanza ------------------------------------- 76
The Serenade -- 77
Snerdle -- 78

Love Endures

Remembrance -- 81
A Love Far Deeper ------------------------------------- 82
The Everlasting Promise ------------------------------ 84

Author's Note

    I didn't go out looking for poetry; rather, it came in search of me on a cold night in January 2024. If I'm being honest, I wasn't sure how this collection would come together. I've never felt "called" to write poetry extensively. However, I've learned that when inspiration visits, it's worth sitting down and spending time with it. So, that's exactly what I did. I vowed to keep writing until this poetic inspiration compelled itself to rest.

    The resulting work is not all the warm clichés love collections promise. Instead, I wanted to tell the story of how love exists among a plethora of sentiments in the background of our lives. I hope you enjoy reading these works as much as I've enjoyed composing them.

With many thanks,
Meg Jaye

INNOCENCE

"The best and most beautiful things in the world cannot be seen or even touched. They must be felt with the heart." - Helen Keller

Nostalgia

Take me back to when
we thrived among gleaming fields
of twilight.
Resplendent fireflies
guiding us like urban sailors
through the flowing dusk-dappled streets.

I want to feel the grass beneath
my earth-worn feet
the roots of nature embracing me
as though I, too, were hugged
by Gaia's verdure-tattooed arms.
A blossom, too
blooming, unadulterated
by worry or purpose.
A time when
everything and nothing
seemed to matter.

Evolution of an Artist

A crayon-wielding toddler
against a freshly painted,
unpigmented wall
sees potential.
There's no method to what he does—
A disaster-colored masterpiece
imbues the wall before him.

A crayon-wielding child
against a freshly painted,
unpigmented wall
sees potential.
Today, he mourns his lost ideas
buried under layers of eggshell white
and draws a rainbow to remind himself
there's always beauty after the storm.

A crayon-wielding adolescent
against a freshly painted,
unpigmented wall
sees potential.
A crowd with scrutinizing eyes
tells him he'll never be good enough—
Fistfuls of scorn scatter
against his motley dappled
musings.

A crayon-wielding young man
against a freshly painted,
unpigmented wall
sees potential.
There's no method to what he does—
A disaster-colored masterpiece
imbues the wall before him.
He raises his arms

defiantly confident to the callous voices—
their criticisms vibrate
with a rumble lacking
in vibrance and vitality.

Their own walls but a tribute
to the desolate conformity
in which they seek solace;
too scared to use color
too scared to be
like him—Standing Out

Unnamed

Hey there, baby boy,

Don't you know you're beautiful?

A piece-by-piece vision

Of love and ambition

A joyous collision

Destiny's celestial star

God's unblinking eye

The boy who wanted to see the world

From the best seat in the Azure Empire

The one no mortal beings can cross

until mortality's hand

ceases us,

carries us,

and guides us.

But you, Little One,

With a light too bright

to ignite this world

to be the fight

the might

the end of darkness in the night.

No, Dear Child, your light

was too perfect to be of this world.

No terrestrial land could possibly make you shine

as brightly as the skies you call home.

We wanted nothing but the world for you, Little One

Yet somehow, you already knew

For you wanted it, too.

But not in a way that anyone knew.

A love that is infinite, eternal

A perpetual spark

painting the journey from dusk to dawn

An eternal love for your eternal journey

One where only you know

what happens next.

CRUSADES

"Love recognizes no barriers. It jumps hurdles, leaps fences, penetrates walls to arrive at its destination full of hope."
-Maya Angelou

The Sunflower

I am the girl who walked through fire.

Bright resilience.

Standing tall.

Always looking towards the sky.

The Queen's Battle Cry

The curling ire of a hurricane
shrieking in power and destruction.

Too proud of her solitary crown
and the unwillingness to share the empire she built
single-handedly,
unmoved
by the jester
who infiltrated under the guise
of magnanimity.

Yet, in truth, he was a descendant
of foolish, ill-begotten, penurious kings
whose wits were found to be as barren
as his gold-starved pockets,
and his joy-desolate existence.

Although a queen's vision can be dimmed
by the stratus woven mists
covering the heavens like a warm winter blanket
Each wish
Each vision
Each memory
remains an eternal reminder of
Everything she was
Everything she is
Everything she will be
no matter the battles
or wayward, drunken travelers
that flood her path
with waves of self-doubt
and illusionary defeat.
The worn-out warrior with
Tired, tear-soaked flesh—
Yet, she persisted.

She is not the queen who forgets her crown.
She does not wait to be rescued
by some chimerical knight
who bears stipulations of
only if
as if only
she's pretty enough
or quiet enough.
But never if
she's wild enough.
or tough enough
or rough enough.
Never if she comes with weapons—
armed with finger-tipped militias
confidently commanded
against the chaos
of knights
unchivalrously guided towards

false idolatries
or fantastic tales
of sacrilegious holy grails.
Their steps are intimidated
by the thunderous roar
of Artemis's impending descent
from the palace of Mount Olympus.
Her goddess shield forged by an unbreakable,
crystallized triumph
imbued with ferrum spiritus —
words that could pierce
the clandestine platinum armor
of these wandering knights
in a single breath.

State of the Nation

Every day is an improvisation.
Some days, it's a celebration,
Others, a defenestration.
That burning sensation
when we cry out
in desperation
because we need a conversation
of transformation
to make our nation
one of adoration.

A combination of inspiration
guided by an incantation.
An administration leading us all
away from temptation.
Abolishing the degradation
of our fractured, severed nation.

We dream of elation —
a united space,

not a senseless place
where compassion is gone
without a trace.

Nourish our World
as a beautiful creation
one where we learn a newfound appreciation
for the innovation and imagination
not for confrontation and agitation
or fanning the flames of alienation.

We drown our silent struggles
craving some quick sensation
wrapped in waves of intoxication
numbing the pain we find
on screens filled with screams
and a world
waiting
for justice
to be
served.

Gentlemen on the Hill

We've been raised among marauders
who call themselves gentlemen.
The mascarade paint,
a miraging façade
obscuring their sanctimonious visages
underneath the spotlight
of a sedentary circus act.

Those ostentatious puppet masters
whose uncut strings stifle our strifes–
burying them
among the bureaucratic
fine print,
as they deliberate our livelihoods
with their incessant "well-wishes"
thrown down
like worn-out pennies in
a wishing well

built along the ruins of old money's
carbon-coated subterranean highways.
Yet they hope thoughts and prayers are enough
to solve everything.

Sagittarius screamed from the cosmos
that we could find absolution
in the solidarity of altruism—
but our ears were too packed
with the ignorant shouts
of suited figures on the high hills—
their outbursts
deafening our chances
for resolution.

Give Them Their Flowers

Give them their flowers —
our brothers and sisters
who rest in power
but not in peace.

Give them strength —
Not just hopes and prayers
that go unanswered
when suffering cries out:
"Hear us" —
only to be met with silence.

Bystanders standing by
with their electronic eyes
unblinking, unmoved
as the River Styx
ties crimson ribbons
around lamp posts,
the cascade of Carmine
rolling endlessly down the sidewalks
where life used to happen.

SPICE

"Life is too important to be taken seriously." - Oscar Wilde

Cacophony's Clutch

Cacophony has caught me—
coughing, choking against
this discordant collection:
the verbal concoction
that swirls around me—
Syncopated serpent,
suffocating
the cadence
of inspiration's fervor.

Ascended

The tears you manifested within me
have ascended
to the heavens of my being.
Victoriously,
I return them to you—
a cataclysmic deluge.

Expiration Date

I took out the trash today.
Piece by piece,
I discarded those memories
I'd kept harbored
in those sentimental cabinets
as though they'd never spoil.
I'd stowed those moments,
the ones I felt most precious,
safely among the boxes of oatmeal and cookies,
thinking, perhaps,
of the honey found in King Tut's tomb,
flavored with the unaged sweetness of eternal love.
Yet finding instead
the rancid smell
of spoiled milk.

Southbound Train

A strong wind blows
and I feel
this sensation—
the interlude to
a final destination.

I can't deny
what's inside.
Memories of time together
severed—
a failed attempt at forever.

This endeavor
but a cue,
a momentary visit—

one that reminds me
there's little to do
but say goodbye.

These emotions
are reaming
through me.
I'm pleading,
depleted.
My mind is retreating,
dragged down—
Time is fleeting.
Waiting for the final stop,
of our terminal meeting.

The Ego's Silent Departure

Memories of your manifestation remind me
how full of hot air you always were.
If only
your inflated ego
were made of something useful
like propane.
Imagine
the places we could have visited,
our feet soaring
above the ground
on the way to some tropical island
scented with the warmth
of perpetual summer.

Instead,
I find remembrance
of your methane-scented spirit
every time I pass Bondi's Island:
A constant reminder that,
although shit happens,
with time
shit also passes.

Amidst the Pieces of the Cerebral Realm

It was all out of order
this discorded disorder.
Caprices—
my mind
crumbled to pieces

These misplaced moments
of validation
longing for moments
of inspiration
when ideas cascade
unafraid,
infiltrate and invade
foraging empires
in the cerebral realm.

But now
all I find is consternation—
an invalidation
where I'm left
in a state of suffocation.

Drowning in the negation,
I raise my hands up
not in resignation,
but praying
for the penetration
of inspiration
to drift into my imagination.

HEALING

"Love is the great miracle cure. Loving ourselves works miracles in our lives."
- Louise L. Hay

Resentment's Reprieve

Walk away —
let me heal the wounds
from the words we've thrown at each other
like daggers
in the epitome
of our own resentments.

Prescription for Healing

I want a world where hurt people
don't hurt people.
Where we find healing
for our hurt feelings
in more than just
a temporary fix.
We need something more
than a mask
which only veils
the symptoms.

Wishes for Redemption

A collision
of decisions
we envision
with renditions of
ambitions
burning up
the opposition.

The ignition
of a vision —
my contrition,
my perdition.
On my knees,
this admission —
Please forgive
my inhibitions.

Lift me up
from these conditions.
Guide me up
up on my mission.

Take my words
as my confession.
Granted me this —
my sweet redemption.

ANTICIPATION

"Anticipation is about hoping for something. Waiting for it. Preparing for it. And dreaming about it." - Ian Bremmer

Searching for Home

Trying to beat this tired feeling
from walking so many miles
lost in exile.
Searching for a place to call my own.
A place to build
my life, my home.

I crave a haven—
some sort of salvation
as I struggle to save myself,
out there
braving life
as life is out there berating me.

These journeys,
all these roads I roam
over mountains, through storms
diving into the great unknown,
have left me wondering
Is there ever truly such a place as home?
A dream where all the roads we've roamed
reveal a treasure worth the endeavors,
a place where everything just comes together?

Shallow Waters

Down in the reeded darkness
obscuring the joy
you once held like a tender wish
wrapped with hopeful breaths,
lurks the eyes that hunt you down—
past visions of past lives
where once you considered yourself
a holy spirit
instead of the holed spirit
you've felt yourself becoming.

Your scorched wings
linger in wait and wonder,
unable to bring yourself

across the seas you've filled
with tenacious melancholy
seeking the promises you made
with both joy and fear.

Time passes
leaving you
wondering
if it's worth the sacrifice.
Do you choose to dive among the depths,
uncertain of the amiability of mermaids
or is it better to remain in the shallows?
Stagnantly aged
but alone;
alive
but never truly feeling
home.

The Odyssey

Getting my life on track
when things
fell through the cracks.
When the pressures
began to stack,
I crumbled,
back
through the cracks
becoming trapped
in a world
under attack.

Sinking through the silence
I found myself alone.
Drowning in the darkness,
desolation was my home.

But this is not my eulogy,
Or cataclysmic ideology.
This, instead,
my odyssey,
The undying fight
to unite me.
The better version
to spite me,
guiding me towards
the right me
of who
I ought to be.

Harvesting Quandaries

I'll tell myself that
I'm doing just fine
trying to get myself unstuck
from the life I've mindlessly laid
stone by stone
hoping to build an Alexandrian empire.

But maybe I'm just wasting time—
maybe it's all just a lie
I devised
to remind myself
of life's temporary nature.

But as the seasons change,
so do I.

Don't worry about me.
Walking aimlessly,
covered in the composted concoctions
of my past misfortunes.

I have a beautiful botanical sanctuary
full of unbloomed aspirations
that I'm watering
with the tears of tomorrow's
"what ifs."

Maybe one day
all of this
will have been
worth it.

DESIRE

"Desire is the starting point of all achievement, not a hope, not a wish, but a keen pulsating desire which transcends everything." - Napoleon Hill

Love's Reverie

I long to hold you
in my arms—
Our star-crossed passions
blurring the line
between dusk and dawn.
Those nights of
eternal paradise,
the crooning tides
serenading us
with their cwtched ebbing.

How I wish
Nychthemeron could conjure
an everlasting grasp
of the heavens above.
I would stroll soundly
through the eternal darkness
If it meant
I could keep you

Forever
by my side.

Yet invariably,
when Apollo's chariot arrives,
you crumble—
those sun-kissed grains
of your being
slip through my fingers,
scattering prismatically
across the shoreline
of the Ethereal Realm.

Our love
but a memory
adrift
with the consciousness
of morning.

Burning Desire

My body is on fire
more than it's ever been.
It's cutting through my deep desires
and burning through my skin.

The words I need to say,
and I need to say them right.
I cannot find the words—
they make me struggle,
make me fight.

In the confines of my mind
Grasping, searching,
There, I find
our feelings intertwined
unextractable—
your heart from mine.

And yet, I am afraid.
If I bare all,
but cannot bear it all
Will you catch me
If I fall?
will you be there
when I call?
Or, in the end,
Will there simply be
nothing there
at all?

The Rapture of Venus

What did I do
to deserve this?
Delivered across my doorstep—
A world I can't contain:
this maniacal madness with
a thing that kills me,
but thrills me—
Venus's unanticipated rapture
capturing the affections
of this avoidant's anxious heart.

For what is this sorcery
that makes it impossible
to extract you from my being?

Trepidation

A serpentine silence
suffocates my soul,
coiling itself around me
in an attempt to stifle
my longing
for you.

Love Pulses

The way you looked at me
With those umber-colored eyes
surrounded by the clouds you carried
lost in serendipitous thought.

Had a stranger stolen my heart so fast
that I couldn't even feel it coming?
Or was it simply some Eros erred-inspired lust
curving onto Cupid's bow
that drew my quivering lips to yours?

Fireflies

I want to breathe you in.
To feel every inch
of your essence
beneath my skin
filling me,
igniting
a bioluminescent irradiation.
Lighting
an enchanted beacon.
Enticing us
intimately closer
with the warmth
of each other's
glow.

Aphrodite's Inferno

Love me at my worst—
I dare you.
Sure, it's a curse.
After all, who would dare to defy logic
by willingly walking through an inferno
expecting to escape unscathed?
Such a spark that sets the soul ablaze—
It must truly be madness
to give someone the power
to destroy everything,
but trusting them implicitly
with every particle of your being.

Cryospheric Atrium

The shirking space
between us
melts.
Flooding the derelict chambers,
those caverns once covered
by a crystalized empire
suffocated by melancholy's
quiescent breath.
It's amazing—
a thing
so empowering,
a thing
so destructive.

SWEET

"Love is the greatest refreshment in life." - Pablo Picasso

Breath of Life: Love's Regeneration

His grief
descended,
devoured by the Night.

In her hands,
the core of his affections,
his lifeblood,
a flood
flowing
across the Paradise
he'd hoped they'd build together.

"Never again," he sobbed in
his dolor drenched
melancholy.

The world around him
spoke of
lateral destiny

and the memories
of love, loss
twinged at his side.
Breath and Life
embodied in not the one he lost
but rather the One
who helped him find
a sacred unity,
a wholeness
he'd somehow lost along the way.
And when she smiled,
he remembered her words:

"I am the light within you;
The love you always carried.
The hope you always needed."

Inked in Sight

Somewhere, sitting
between the lines
you'll find
me—
embedded in the words
you'd passed by
a hundred times,
swearing you knew them
verbatim.
In hindsight,
realizing
you'd only skimmed the surface.

Perhaps things had changed
when life gave you new translations,
new perspectives.

Only then,
you remembered
to return
with renewed eyes
and a reminiscent heart
because you longed
for answers.
Believing you'd find them
when you retraced your steps
among the inked impressions.

Persephone's Dream

I followed you
to the edges of the universe.
My passions bloomed
a perpetual spring
of fancied floras
paving the way
to the threshold
of your heart.

Instead
I found myself
At the entrance
to your immortal tomb;
"A tribute," you say,
"to the ever-lasting life
that love infuses
through every corner
of the astral-painted cosmos."

Intrepidly,
I approach
the boundless permanence,
knowing we'll forever dance
when the autumn leaves
descend upon the earth.

Wanted

The flaws of your figure
finessed with the dew
of your labors,
glistening along your youth-starved flesh.

Your eccentricities—
The way you lose yourself
in the solitude of dusk's
journey into nightfall
with the rumbles of slumber
vibrating your weary bones.

Unaware
that I would choose
your existence
Every time.

Morning Jazz

Five fingers curled around a white porcelain trophy,
a tribute to the day ahead.
That swirling potion of magic beans,
a swarthy portal of unuttered confessions.
Its unbiased ear waits, eager to listen.
Your lips pursed against its edges.

An unfaltering sweetness
which penetrates the soul,
uplifting you beyond
that simple mahogany pool.
Dancing to the enchanted words of an ancient spell
with words that contain something sacred.
Yet only sometimes do they seep out
when you carry your cup,
somewhere between sleep and consciousness's doorstep.

I promised not to ask you for the key.
The one that turns on the music box
with your life's magnum opus.
But that was before I imagined it:
Those auditory fireworks.
A Kaleidoscope of loquacious elocutions
you'd loved to scatter
across the table over breakfast.
If only it were years ago
and only it stopped feeling
too late to rouse the band
who always seemed to know the right song to play
to awaken a cardiac melody
whenever those troublesome butterflies
filled every corner of your life
during those adolescence springs
that seemed to drag on for decades.

In the wrong hands, those sentiments became
bombastic adulations,
a smoldering reminder
of everything you loved
and everything they took from you.

"The lock didn't used to be there," you said.
It happened once you discovered
you carried something so intricately valuable
yet nearly impossible to keep whole.
You'd leave it playing nightly
with the dancers and musicians
gliding to every word as if to show
the incessant beauty and amorosity
you felt defined the essence of life.
Then you found it.
A passion packed with nitroglycerin.
A word that shuddered past your lips:

"Love," you said, "An
Opulent and
Virulently vivacious
Existence."

You took another sip,
remembering beneath the sweetness
there's always a hint
of bitterness.

Autumn Esperanza

Your golden honey spirit
adorns the embers of
my tattered existence.
Ascending the sky,
wrapped in chromatic splendor,
you carry the rain,
but make me rise
like flowers in spring.

The Serenade

Your voice stretches
as though crafted from velvet twine
twisting endlessly,
weaving a comforting notion
that warms the mind and spirit
as though igniting summer's passions
through the fibers between us,
waiting for lyrics to descend from the heavens
knowing, however,
the heavens are closer than they appear.

In impetus's shadow,
the zealous musicians
poised with strings engaged,
percussions placed
play an array of harmonies and cadences
that guide us
across the boundlessness
of imagination.

Snerdle

Hold off the day a little longer
as morning peers,
slowly gliding along the sky.
Its embrace tempting,
yet not as comforting
as that momentary bliss
you find cradled among
the silken comforter
dazzled with the last bits
of slumber's serenity.

LOVE ENDURES

"True love stories never have endings." - Richard Bach

Remembrance

I thought of you today.
The echoes of your memory
playing in my ears—
A wistful reminder
of how quickly
time becomes but a memory,
one where we desperately
try to hold the pieces together
as the days fold
one into another.

A Love Far Deeper
For Yuko and Yasuo

The ends of the earth will not stop me from finding you.
How do I begin to live, to truly live, without you?
Sometimes, I pause, hoping to hear your voice carried along the wind,
sending me a signal or whisper of where I might find you.
Yet, too often, I am only greeted
with the cries of lost souls
searching, too, for safe passage to the celestial sea
bridge of Ame-no-umi.

The infinite layers tell us to look beyond our existence,
to swim incessantly against the currents.
Because love is so much stronger than Poseidon's wrath;
that thief who stole the pearl—my pearl— from my grasp.

Time wears my bones,
but never my love for you.

I will carry it with me,
albeit soaked from the salted waters
where I've tirelessly searched,
longing to bring you home,
holding tightly to the promise I made to you
in that last exchange we shared
so very long ago.

When the Shinigami brings my one-way ticket
to the far ends of this life,
I can only hope it includes the chance
to take you once more as my bride,
carrying you across the threshold
over Ame-no-umi
with a ceremonial embrace
as eternal lovers among the deities.

The Everlasting Promise
For my soulmate

Here is to a lifetime to share.
Not just for as we are now
but for whom we will continue to become
as we senesce across this life together.

When we need each other most,
may our endearing love
guide us where we need to be.
When our life's light seems to have dimmed,
because the fire's fuel has dwindled down
I promise
we will find a way to rekindle our passions
together.

May humor always reside
within these four walls of our home,
But not entombed within them.

Humor deserves a life of its own,
as a cheerful ghost
haunting our home in its own smug little way.
Perhaps it will sneak in silently during a spontaneous date night
as though we'd hired a band of tuba players
whose laughter undulates through the brass horns
failing to attempt a love ballad,
but succeeding in making us laugh until our sides hurt.

One day,
we will not be the same people standing
before each other.
The passage of time
will have won the battle
against both of us.
But I will, nevertheless,
cherish you
as our love will evolve
again and again
through light and darkness.

Should we wake up
as if we're strangers meeting for the first time
over breakfast in our kitchen,
may we still see that magic
that makes love
so incredibly special.

I vow to remain
Your lover and companion
Side by side
In hope and despair
In happiness and sorrow
Through anything and everything
With a love that will
Strengthen and endure.

To always
find a way back
to each other
in both this life,
and the next.

www.ingramcontent.com/pod-product-compliance
Lightning Source LLC
Chambersburg PA
CBHW052150070526
44585CB00017B/2058